MW01423743

What Is Your Story?

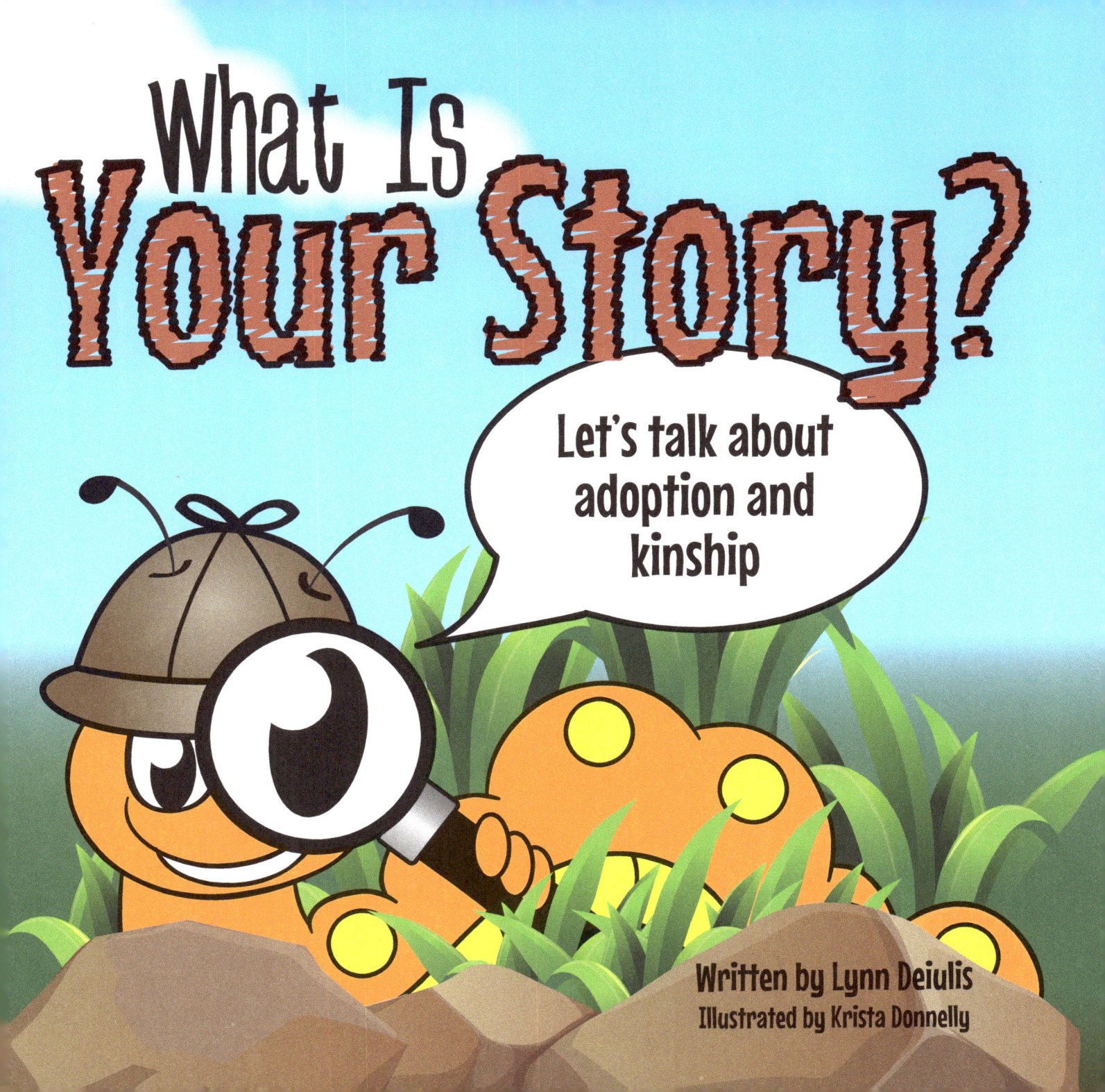

Let's talk about adoption and kinship

Written by Lynn Deiulis
Illustrated by Krista Donnelly

◆ FriesenPress

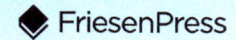

One Printers Way
Altona, MB R0G0B0
Canada

www.friesenpress.com

Copyright © 2021 by Lynn Deiulis
First Edition — 2021

All rights reserved.

No part of this publication may be reproduced in any form, or by any means, electronic or mechanical, including photocopying, recording, or any information browsing, storage, or retrieval system, without permission in writing from FriesenPress.

Graphic design and illustrations by Krista Donnelly

ISBN
978-1-03-911779-2 (Hardcover)
978-1-03-911778-5 (Paperback)
978-1-03-911780-8 (eBook)

Juvenile Nonfiction, Family, Adoption

Distributed to the trade by The Ingram Book Company

INTRODUCTION

This book uses butterflies, caterpillars, and other insects to illustrate the many ways adoptive and kinship stories are created. You might find bits of your story in this book but not your whole story. There are as many types of birth parents as there are types of butterflies! There are as many types of families as there are types of plants! There are as many stories of how children came to be living with their families as there are stars in the sky! But there is only one **you**, and **your story** is as unique as you are.

Let's get reading!

Everyone who reads this book with you, or the people you talk with about the questions in this book, will be able to help you learn about **your story**. That's because although they may be a part of your story, you are the **STAR!**

Chapter 1: The Egg Story

When a grown-up female butterfly is ready to make new butterflies, she produces eggs. A male butterfly fertilizes these eggs. Then the female butterfly adds a very, very, very sticky glue that helps keep her eggs stuck to a leaf. She does this to keep the eggs safe from bad weather and so that when the eggs hatch into caterpillars, they can eat the leaf right away. The butterfly carefully plans where the eggs will be glued to a good, healthy leaf, but she does not stay there to wait for the eggs to hatch.

Guess what?

You started out as an egg too, but a human egg, not a butterfly egg, and you are certainly not a caterpillar!

Human eggs need to be fertilized too! People usually call the person who fertilizes the egg a **birth father** or **biological father**.

Fertilized human eggs grow into babies inside of a **birth mother** or **biological mother** instead of on a leaf. Sometimes she is called a tummy mommy, a first mother, or a surrogate mother.

Sometimes people even call your birth or biological mother your **real mother**. WHAT? When someone says your **real mother**, or **real father** they usually mean your birth parents.

By working together to fertilize the egg, your birth mother and birth father gave you gifts that you will always have from them. These gifts include things like your hair colour, skin colour, eye colour, and how tall or short you will be when you grow up. Sometimes these gifts help you to be good at things like singing, running, or drawing pictures! You might think of these as genetic gifts because you received them when you were born.

Sometimes social workers write this kind of information in a social and medical history, or a life book, so that your **new family** can know what genetic traits your birth parents had. This will help your new family recognize those genetic gifts in **you**.

Let's Talk!

Who can you talk with about all these names for the person who gave birth to you?

What does your family call **your** biological or birth parent(s)?

When you think of **your** "real" mother, who do you picture?

Who can you talk with that can help you figure out what genetic gifts your birth parents gave to you?

straight hair
short
tall
brown eyes
blue eyes
artistic
funny

Activity Time: Chapter 1 Word Search

Word List

- BABIES
- BOOK
- EGGS
- FATHER
- FERTILIZE
- FUNNY
- GENETICS
- GLUE
- LEAF
- LIFE
- MOTHER
- PLANT
- SHORT
- TALL

```
K K F K N B G L U E F B E T
L E A F P F J Y Y A V O R V
W L M D N L E H D R S O W Q
P L O L C W A R Q N H K O Q
F A T H E R Z N T S E U V R
U M H E G E N E T I C S L M
W S E G H K L W R F L K V J
N L R G U S W X B A B I E S
L D I S X F E B N O E H Z E
A G W F R I E Q M T A L L E
F U V S E H C Y F U N N Y J
```

Activity Time: **Chapter 1 Drawing**

Draw a picture of something you are good at!

Chapter 2: Where To Put The Egg?

Maybe your birth parent(s) put hard work and energy into trying to keep you on your birth leaf, just like a butterfly's egg glue, or maybe your birth parent(s) struggled with grown-up stuff. Maybe social workers, lawyers, and a judge had to make a very, very hard decision. They may have had to decide if you could be healthy staying on a leaf on your birth family plant or if they had to find you a new family plant. This is because eggs and caterpillars need healthy leaves where they can hatch and grow into the best butterflies they can be.

Maybe your birth parent(s) planned to find a healthy leaf somewhere on the birth family plant where they thought you could hatch safely and grow from a caterpillar into a healthy butterfly. This strong, healthy leaf might have belonged to a grandparent, cousin, aunt, or uncle. It might have been on a family friend's plant, or even a leaf on a plant in your cultural community's garden. If they picked a leaf on your birth family's plant, this is usually called a **kinship placement**. This is also sometimes called **customary care** or even **legal guardianship**.

Sometimes birth parents' own family plants could not give an egg or a caterpillar what they needed to become a healthy butterfly because the family plants were older or did not have strong leaves. Sometimes the other leaves on the birth family plants were not any healthier than the birth parents'

Who can you talk with about this?

Hon. E. Bee

leaves. Therefore, a leaf on the birth family plant may not have been the right place for your egg to hatch into a caterpillar and grow into the best butterfly possible.

Sometimes birth parents did not even look for leaves on their family plant because they wanted their egg to have their start on a completely new family plant.

Maybe your new parent(s) needed help placing an egg on their leaf, and your birth parent(s) wanted to help them.

Adoption is when birth parents and social workers look at leaves on many other family plants to pick out the one that they think is the best match for the egg. Sometimes foster care and kinship placements can turn into adoption too!

Let's Talk!

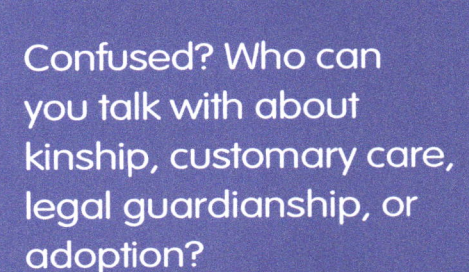

Confused? Who can you talk with about kinship, customary care, legal guardianship, or adoption?

Maybe **your** egg story is very different from these stories.

Who can you talk with about **your** egg story?

Which one is the best match?

Activity Time: Chapter 2 Word Search

Word List

GARDENS
KINSHIP
JUDGE
FAMILY
TOYS
MATCHING
ADOPTION
BIKE
GLUE
COMMUNITY
SIBLINGS
DECISION
COUSINS

A	S	I	B	L	I	N	G	S	F	T	T	J	P
D	K	N	B	Q	D	E	C	I	S	I	O	N	K
O	Q	W	C	I	G	L	U	E	T	S	P	J	I
P	G	E	P	O	S	A	M	R	C	L	C	U	N
T	O	Y	S	F	M	E	R	O	U	U	P	D	S
I	Y	D	K	E	G	M	R	D	K	D	G	H	
O	B	I	K	E	R	Q	U	H	E	S	X	E	I
N	C	M	A	T	C	H	I	N	G	N	C	E	P
F	A	M	I	L	Y	I	Y	A	I	Q	S	N	O
G	R	A	N	D	P	A	R	E	N	T	S	E	S
D	B	A	J	C	O	U	S	I	N	S	Y	W	L

Activity Time: **Chapter 2 Drawing**

Draw some healthy plants in a garden!

Chapter 3: The Waiting Leaf

Sometimes, while birth families, social workers, lawyers, and judges make a plan to find the best plant for the egg, the egg is glued onto a special waiting leaf. This waiting leaf might be a **foster family**, also sometimes called a **resource family**. It can be very confusing on this waiting leaf because eggs from other butterflies are glued on the waiting leaf too. Sometimes eggs move to a new plant right away, but sometimes eggs stay on a waiting leaf for a long time.

Instead of a foster family, the egg might be glued onto a waiting leaf on the birth family plant while a new plan is being made. Remember, this is called a **kinship placement**.

Sometimes it looks like a giant spider web connecting all these leaves and plants to each other while everyone is looking for the best leaf for the egg where it can hatch into a caterpillar and grow into a healthy butterfly.

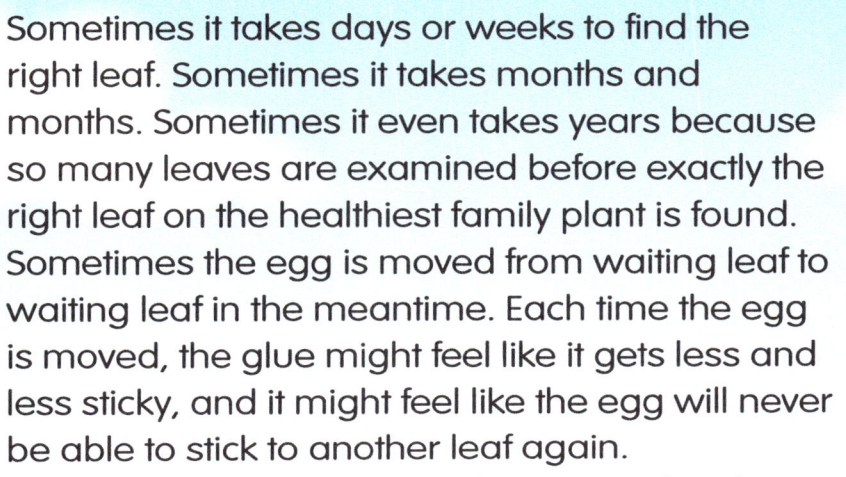

Sometimes it takes days or weeks to find the right leaf. Sometimes it takes months and months. Sometimes it even takes years because so many leaves are examined before exactly the right leaf on the healthiest family plant is found. Sometimes the egg is moved from waiting leaf to waiting leaf in the meantime. Each time the egg is moved, the glue might feel like it gets less and less sticky, and it might feel like the egg will never be able to stick to another leaf again.
However, once a strong leaf on a new family plant is found, the egg will be moved from its waiting leaf to the new leaf where it can stick, hatch into a healthy caterpillar, and become the best butterfly it can be!

Let's Talk!

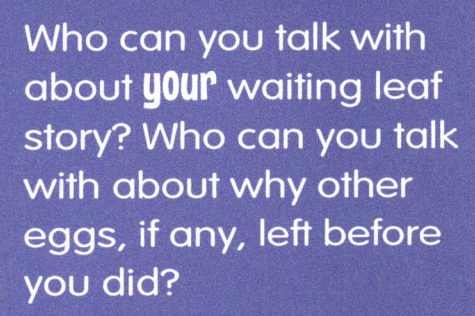

Who can you talk with about **your** waiting leaf story? Who can you talk with about why other eggs, if any, left before you did?

Who can you ask if **you** had one or more placements between your birth family and your new family?

Activity Time: Chapter 3 Word Search

Word List

WAITING
FOSTER
LAWYER
FAMILY
KINSHIP
MOVING
STICKY
RESOURCE
PLACEMENTS
ADOPTION
FRIENDS
CONFUSING
SUITCASE
FEELINGS

R	E	S	O	U	R	C	E	G	G	D	V	W	J
C	P	C	O	N	F	U	S	I	N	G	F	A	T
G	L	A	C	Y	F	M	P	V	S	V	R	I	G
T	A	D	Y	Z	O	O	U	B	T	K	I	T	C
I	C	O	S	F	S	V	L	Q	I	I	E	I	A
N	E	P	N	A	T	I	A	N	C	N	N	N	C
P	M	T	G	M	E	N	W	G	K	S	D	G	T
U	E	I	Q	I	R	G	Y	E	Y	H	S	K	C
S	N	O	L	L	P	F	E	E	L	I	N	G	S
K	T	N	X	Y	R	F	R	Z	S	P	H	H	T
U	S	U	I	T	C	A	S	E	W	F	E	W	X

Activity Time: **Chapter 3 Drawing**

Draw a spider web!

CHAPTER 4: Learning from Our Families

Did you know that butterflies fly from somewhere cool to somewhere hot every year? They travel great distances to avoid the cold. For generations their ancestors have done this. Butterflies do not do well in cold weather; in fact, many of them cannot even fly in the cold.

Many human birth families have traditions that go back for generations too. Traditions include things like creating amazing patterns on clothing with beads, chewing on raw sugar cane, using henna dye to create patterns on skin, travelling on dogsleds, eating food with chopsticks, and many other things, such as religious traditions and practices from all over the world.

You might think of traditions learned while living within your family or community as **cultural gifts**. Often these traditions include skills that you can use for the rest of your life.

Earlier we talked about the **genetic gifts** your birth parents gave you that you were born with and that you will have for life. Butterflies get their wing colour and style from their birth parents. That is a genetic gift example.
If, instead of instinct, butterflies learned how to glue their eggs to plant leaves by watching other butterflies, that would be a cultural gift example.

As we talked about before, when a person cannot grow up with their birth parent(s) sometimes grandparents, aunts, uncles, cousins, or the birth family's community will present a plan to take care of them. This way the birth family can make sure there are opportunities for their children to learn their cultural traditions and pass them on from generation to generation.

When matching the egg with a leaf on another family plant, the social workers try to get as much information as possible about the birth family's cultural and religious history. Then they include it in a social and medical history or life book. This is so the new family can learn and share what traditions and religious beliefs the birth parent(s) and their families had.

Let's Talk!

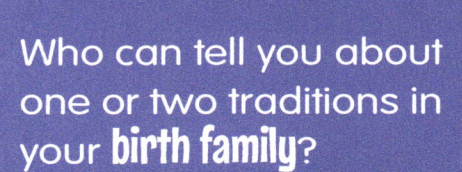

Who can tell you about one or two traditions in your **birth family**?

Who can tell you about one or two traditions in your **new family**?

Guess what?

Sometimes your new family and your birth family even have some of the same traditions!

L.D. BUGG

Activity Time: Chapter 4 Word Search

Word List

TRADITIONS
SKILLS
FAMILY
ADOPTION
GENETIC
GIFTS
LEARNING
BUILDING
COMMUNITY
LIFEBOOK
HISTORY
RELIGION
CULTURE
KINSHIP

T	R	E	L	I	G	I	O	N	Y	M	T	M	I
H	N	U	T	C	V	O	A	O	E	L	F	L	K
Q	Y	L	R	L	I	F	E	B	O	O	K	C	Z
A	B	U	A	D	C	O	M	M	U	N	I	T	Y
D	U	G	D	S	N	P	O	Q	R	I	N	L	Q
O	I	I	I	K	K	I	N	S	H	I	P	W	J
P	L	F	T	I	L	E	A	R	N	I	N	G	I
T	D	T	I	L	G	E	N	E	T	I	C	R	N
I	I	S	O	L	U	I	C	U	L	T	U	R	E
O	N	H	N	S	B	R	H	I	S	T	O	R	Y
N	G	V	S	W	L	I	F	A	M	I	L	Y	U

Activity Time: **Chapter 4 Drawing**

Draw a picture of a tradition that you like!

CHAPTER 5: Questions About Your Story

Sometimes there are no leaves on the birth family plant, on any family friends' plants, or in cultural community gardens able to take care of an egg. Even though everyone examined all the leaves on all the plants, they could not find the right match for the egg.

Remember, there are as many reasons for this as there are kinds of butterflies. Usually, grown-up stuff makes it too hard for the leaves on these plants to be able to take care of an egg.

Guess what?

Not one of these reasons was your egg's fault, but sometimes it might feel that way!

Let's Talk!

Who can you talk with about anything you think **your** egg might have done to have to leave **your** birth plant?

Who can you talk with about the reasons **you** needed a new family?

Don't forget that you're still connected to your birth family by genetics. Remember the genetic gifts they gave you? That connection will never change.

You are also connected to your adoptive or kinship family by creating new family traditions and memories together!

Guess what?
You might even remember some of the times you spent with your birth family members! Life books help us remember such things.

Guess what?
Did you know that it's okay to be connected to more than one family? Sometimes we even build connections with our adoptive or kinship families and still keep in touch with birth family members!

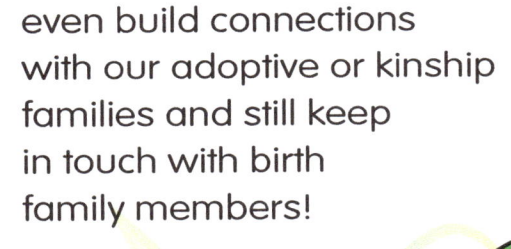

Let's Talk!

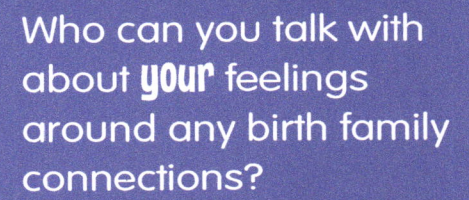

Who can you talk with about **your** feelings around any birth family connections?

Who can tell you if you have a life book and help you see it?

Who can tell you if you have a social and medical history and when you will be old enough to read it?

Activity Time: Chapter 5 Word Search

Word List

- CARING
- REASONS
- FAMILY
- KINSHIP
- FAULT
- QUESTIONS
- MOVING
- FEELINGS
- CONNECTIONS
- LIFEBOOK
- MEMORIES
- GIFTS
- CULTURE
- ADOPTION

```
G A O M K I N S H I P Y Q R
I F A M I L Y A B F P L U E
F W Y L K D I D K E Q I E A
T N N T N Q M O Z E P F S S
S W Y D V H B P J L I E T O
C U L T U R E T S I E B I N
C O N N E C T I O N S O O S
E Q E U G W R O P G T O N K
X C J C A R I N G S D K S U
Z U C R Z I M E M O R I E S
F A U L T B A Q M O V I N G
```

Activity Time: **Chapter 5 Drawing**

Draw some activities that you like to do with your family!

CHAPTER 6: You are the STAR

So, for some reason, you had to leave your birth parents' care. Then you started **your own story** where you are the STAR.

Maybe you moved to a foster/resource home for a little while where you learned some new traditions and skills, like how to cook certain foods.
Who can tell you about that foster/resource home? Do you have a favourite food or tradition from living there?

Maybe you moved to a kinship home for a little while where you learned some family traditions and skills. Who can tell you about that kinship home? Do you have a favourite food or tradition from living there?

Maybe you moved in with a community member, and you are growing up with your birth family members around you. Maybe they are teaching you skills and traditions that you can teach someone else one day.
Who can tell you what one or more of these traditions are?
Do you have a favourite one?

Maybe you moved to a family that wants to adopt you or already has adopted you, where you are learning new traditions and skills as you are growing up.
Who can tell you what one or more of these traditions are?
Do you have a favourite one?

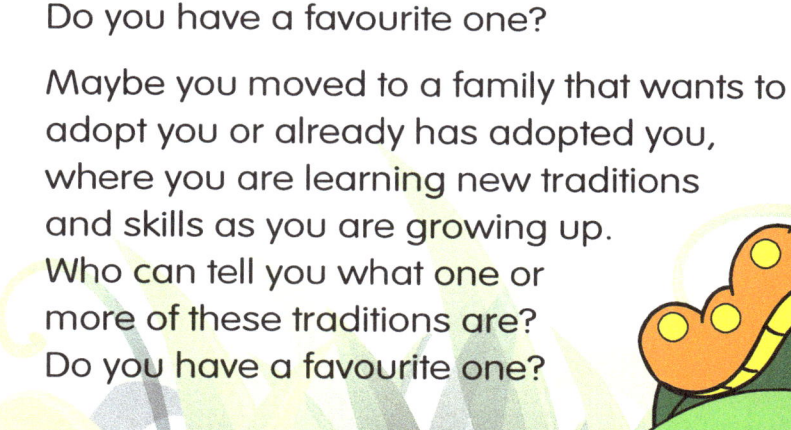

Maybe you still visit with birth family members sometimes, write letters to them, or talk on the phone with them about the things you do while you are apart.

Remember when we talked about butterflies that travel every year from somewhere cold to somewhere hot? Every year the butterflies return, and many are reunited with their grown-up butterfly children. Maybe they talk with each other about what has happened while they were apart.

One day when you are a grown up, you might be able to meet your birth family members, and then all of you can talk with each other about what happened while you were apart.

Remember, talking to someone you trust is the best way to learn about YOUR story!

Let's Talk!

Who can you talk with about how you feel about having contact with birth family members now, or about seeing them in the future?

Who can you talk with about the rights you will have when you turn eighteen years old?

Who can you talk with about any feelings you might have from reading the stories in this book?

Activity Time: Chapter 6 Word Search

Word List

- STAR
- TRADITIONS
- GENETICS
- FAMILY
- KINSHIP
- ADOPTION
- QUESTIONS
- MOVING
- FEELINGS
- CONTACT
- REUNION
- MEMORIES
- FAVOURITES
- BUTTERFLY

B	D	U	P	N	M	E	M	O	R	I	E	S	W
N	F	O	T	R	A	D	I	T	I	O	N	S	Z
Q	F	E	E	L	I	N	G	S	M	S	L	T	F
U	G	K	I	N	S	H	I	P	F	T	L	W	L
E	M	G	E	N	E	T	I	C	S	A	N	S	W
S	O	I	F	F	F	A	V	O	U	R	I	T	E
T	V	V	A	D	O	P	T	I	O	N	Y	V	O
I	I	K	M	C	O	N	T	A	C	T	S	V	K
O	N	W	I	V	F	R	E	U	N	I	O	N	Q
N	G	C	L	Z	K	E	P	U	B	Q	I	D	J
S	R	C	Y	B	U	T	T	E	R	F	L	Y	D

Activity Time: **Chapter 6 Drawing**

Draw a picture of what you want to do when you grow up!

Now, this is your spot for writing down any questions you might have that we did not think of!

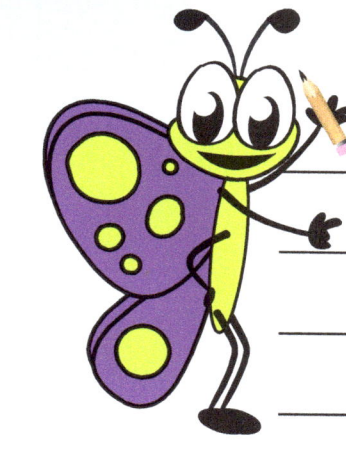

Let's Talk!

Who can you discuss your questions with?

Word Search Answer Page

CHAPTER 1

K	K	F	K	N	B	G	L	U	E	F	B	E	T
L	E	A	F	P	F	J	Y	Y	A	V	O	R	V
W	L	M	D	N	L	E	H	D	R	S	O	W	Q
P	L	O	L	C	W	A	R	Q	N	H	K	O	Q
F	A	T	H	E	R	Z	N	T	S	E	U	V	R
U	M	H	E	G	E	N	E	T	I	C	S	L	M
W	S	E	G	H	K	L	W	R	F	L	K	V	J
N	L	R	G	U	S	W	X	B	A	B	I	E	S
L	D	I	S	X	F	E	B	N	O	E	H	Z	E
A	G	W	F	R	I	E	Q	M	T	A	L	L	E
F	U	V	S	E	H	C	Y	F	U	N	N	Y	J

CHAPTER 2

A	S	I	B	L	I	N	G	S	F	T	T	J	P
D	K	N	B	Q	D	E	C	I	S	I	O	N	K
O	Q	W	C	I	G	L	U	E	T	S	P	J	I
P	G	E	P	O	S	A	M	R	C	L	C	U	N
T	O	Y	S	F	M	E	R	O	U	U	P	D	S
I	Y	D	K	E	G	M	R	D	K	D	D	G	H
O	B	I	K	E	R	Q	U	H	E	S	X	E	I
N	C	M	A	T	C	H	I	N	G	N	C	E	P
F	A	M	I	L	Y	I	Y	A	I	Q	S	N	O
G	R	A	N	D	P	A	R	E	N	T	S	E	S
D	B	A	J	C	O	U	S	I	N	S	Y	W	L

CHAPTER 3

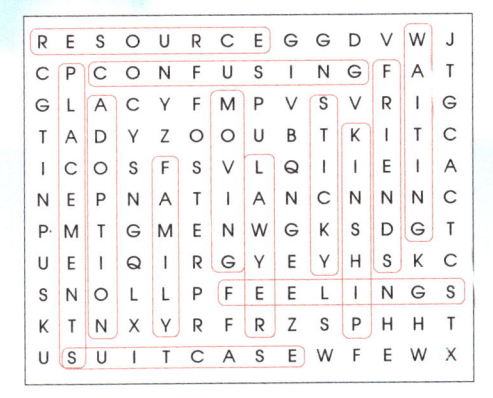

R	E	S	O	U	R	C	E	G	G	D	V	W	J
C	P	C	O	N	F	U	S	I	N	G	F	A	I
G	L	A	C	Y	F	M	P	V	S	V	R	I	T
T	A	D	Y	Z	O	O	U	B	T	K	I	T	I
I	C	O	S	F	S	V	L	Q	I	I	E	I	N
N	E	P	N	A	T	I	A	N	C	N	N	N	G
P	M	T	G	M	E	N	W	G	K	S	D	G	C
U	E	I	Q	I	R	G	Y	E	Y	H	S	K	T
S	N	O	L	L	P	F	E	E	L	I	N	G	S
K	T	N	X	Y	F	R	Z	S	P	H	H	C	C
U	S	U	I	T	C	A	S	E	W	F	E	W	X

CHAPTER 4

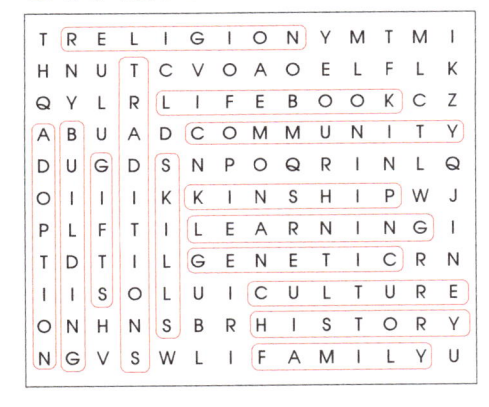

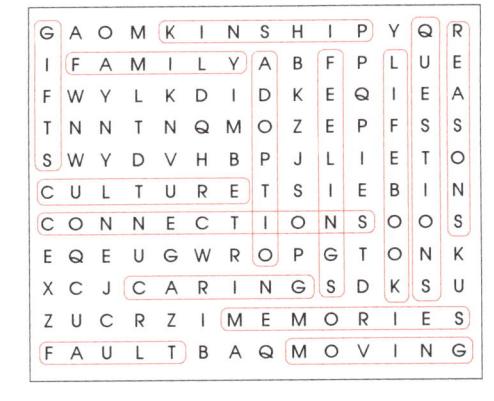

T	R	E	L	I	G	I	O	N	Y	M	T	M	I
H	N	U	T	C	V	O	A	O	E	L	F	L	K
Q	Y	L	R	L	I	F	E	B	O	O	K	C	Z
A	B	U	A	D	C	O	M	M	U	N	I	T	Y
D	U	G	D	S	N	P	O	Q	R	I	N	L	Q
O	I	G	I	K	K	I	N	S	H	I	P	W	J
P	L	F	T	I	L	E	A	R	N	I	N	G	I
T	D	T	I	L	G	E	N	E	T	I	C	R	N
I	I	S	O	L	U	I	C	U	L	T	U	R	E
O	N	H	N	S	B	R	H	I	S	T	O	R	Y
N	G	V	S	W	L	I	F	A	M	I	L	Y	U

CHAPTER 5

G	A	O	M	K	I	N	S	H	I	P	Y	Q	R
I	F	A	M	I	L	Y	A	B	F	P	L	U	E
F	W	Y	L	K	D	I	D	K	E	Q	I	E	A
T	N	N	T	N	Q	M	O	Z	E	P	F	S	S
S	W	Y	O	V	H	B	P	J	L	I	E	T	O
C	U	L	T	U	R	E	T	S	I	E	B	I	N
C	O	N	N	E	C	T	I	O	N	S	O	O	S
E	Q	E	U	G	W	R	O	P	G	T	O	N	K
X	C	J	C	A	R	I	N	G	S	D	K	S	U
Z	U	C	R	Z	I	M	E	M	O	R	I	E	S
F	A	U	L	T	B	A	Q	M	O	V	I	N	G

CHAPTER 6

B	D	U	P	N	M	E	M	O	R	I	E	S	W
N	F	O	T	R	A	D	I	T	I	O	N	S	Z
Q	F	E	E	L	I	N	G	S	M	S	L	T	F
U	G	K	I	N	S	H	I	P	F	T	L	W	L
E	M	G	E	N	E	T	I	C	S	A	N	S	W
S	O	I	F	F	A	V	O	U	R	I	T	E	T
T	V	V	A	D	O	P	T	I	O	N	Y	V	O
I	I	K	M	C	O	N	T	A	C	T	S	V	K
O	N	W	I	V	F	R	E	U	N	I	O	N	Q
N	G	C	L	Z	K	E	P	U	B	Q	I	D	J
S	R	C	Y	B	U	T	T	E	R	F	L	Y	D

27

What Is: Her Story

Lynn Deiulis was placed on adoption at the age of nine months in 1960. Her adoptive parents were advised to raise her as their own and forget where she had come from. Her parents followed this advice, and adoption became an uncomfortable topic. Her mother would answer Lynn's adoption questions, but the emotion in her mother's eyes eventually made Lynn stop asking. Lynn grew up not knowing how or whom to ask her many questions. As an adult, Lynn found and met some of her paternal and maternal birth family members and was able to learn much about the genetic and familial information she grew up without. As a result, she has been able to piece together more of her story.

Lynn holds a Bachelor of Arts in Child and Youth Care and enjoyed a twenty-five year career in adoption services. Lynn has worked with many members of the adoption triad (children, birth parents, adoptive parents) as well as foster care and kinship families. She co-facilitated support groups where adult adopted persons, and birth parents, could freely share their unique stories and learn how and where to get some of their questions answered. Her personal and professional journey sparked a passion to write a book that offers an opportunity for children to learn the unique details of their adoption or kinship stories, and helps adults talk to children about how they came to be living together as a family or living with another family. She also hopes the book will help professionals who work with children living through all phases of the adoption or kinship journey. Lynn resides in Northern Ontario, where she enjoys spending time with her husband and family, especially her grandchildren.

What Is: Their Story

The relationship between the author and the illustrator has a unique quality. Krista Donnelly and Lynn are birth half sisters who met each other as adults in 2018. Separated by the adoption process, Krista and her three full sisters grew up not knowing that two older half sisters existed. When Lynn decided to write this book, she reached out to her "new sister" who is a talented graphic designer. Krista brought the book's characters to life while building a relationship with Lynn at the same time. Krista learned about the impact on Lynn of growing up as an adoptee, while Lynn learned about the impact on Krista of discovering she had two birth half sisters she never knew existed! Their new mutual understanding of the impact of adoption has enriched this book.

Lynn and Krista hope this book will help children and families talk about these unique stories long before the children become adults.

CPSIA information can be obtained
at www.ICGtesting.com
Printed in the USA
LVHW071400200122
708999LV00009B/784

9 781039 117792